Declarations to Speak Life Over Your Children

Nurturing Identity, Purpose and Wisdom Through God's Word

Christy Ojikutu

An Intentional Spiritual Parenting Declaration Series Book 1

Declarations to Speak Life Over Your Children
Nurturing Identity, Purpose and Wisdom Through
God's Word

Copyright© 2025 by Christy Ojikutu

Unless otherwise noted, Scripture quotations are taken
from the New King James Version®.Copyright ©
1982 by Thomas Nelson. Used by permission. All
rights reserved

Published by WhollyBooks
Whollybooks.com

ISBN 978-1-968787-02-8 (pbk)
ISBN 978-1-968787-03-5 (eBook)

Printed in the United States of America

Table of Contents

About This Series

This book is part of the **Intentional Spiritual Parenting Declaration** series—a collection of **stand-alone, scripture-based guides** created to help parents raise children with faith, purpose, and biblical vision.

Each book focuses on a unique aspect of spiritual parenting and can be read **independently** or in **any order**. Whether you're starting here or continuing the journey, each title is packed with declarations, biblical truths, and practical insights to help you parent with spiritual clarity and confidence.

Books in the Series: Include

1. Declarations to Speak Life Over Your Children — Nurturing Identity, Purpose, and Wisdom Through God's Word

2. Declarations to Speak Life Over Your Children — Nurturing Wellness, Courage, and Character Through God's Word

3. Declarations to Speak Life Over Your Children — Nurturing Leadership, Impact and Authority in the Seven Mountains of Influence Through God's Word

(More titles too!)

Look for the **Intentional Spiritual Parenting Declaration** series label on each title to easily identify books in this collection.

Preface

As parents, we are entrusted with one of the greatest privileges: shaping the lives of the next generation. The words we speak over our children hold the potential to unlock their God-given destinies. This book is a call to partner with God in speaking life over our children and our families. The power of spoken promises — declarations grounded in God's Word — can transform not only our children but also our homes, our marriages, and our lives. This guide is designed to help parents speak identity, purpose, and wisdom into their children's hearts every day.

Each day's declaration is backed by Scripture, ensuring that what we speak aligns with God's perfect will for our families. May this guide become a tool in your daily spiritual practice and a powerful reminder that your words have the ability to shape the future.

Acknowledgments

I want to express my deepest thanks to God—His wisdom, grace, and unfailing love have carried me through every step of this journey. His presence has been my strength, and His Word my guide.

I'm also grateful for the family, friends, and mentors who prayed, encouraged, and supported me along the way. Your kindness and faith have meant more than you know.

Finally, thank you to the parents, grandparents, and caregivers who will take these words and speak life over their children. You are the reason this book was written. May God bless you richly as you declare His promises in your home.

Dedication

To every parent who dares to believe God's promises over their children: may your words build worlds of faith, hope, and destiny. This book is lovingly dedicated to you, your children, and the generations yet to come.

Introduction

Words carry tremendous power. Proverbs 18:21 tells us that "Death and life are in the power of the tongue." As parents, our words have the authority to shape, nurture, and call forth the God-given destinies of our children.

Declarations are not mere positive affirmations; they are the living, breathing Word of God applied intentionally over our children's lives. When we declare Scripture, we align our hearts—and theirs—with heaven's truth, planting seeds that will bear fruit for a lifetime.

This book focuses on important truths (identity, purpose, wisdom, etc) that every child needs to grow into the person God created them to be. For example, understanding their true identity — who they are in God's eyes — gives them a foundation of security, worth, and confidence in God. Next, discovering their purpose helps them know why they are here and how they can make a difference.

Finally, wisdom shows them how to walk out that purpose with care, courage, and clarity. All of this, and more, is grounded in the timeless guidance of God's Word, which provides the direction and strength parents need to nurture these qualities in their children.

The book will equip you to speak identity, purpose, wisdom, protection,, victory, and healthy relationships over your children. Use it daily. Speak boldly. Believe deeply. Watch as God's Word transforms your home, your children, and even your own heart.

1
Identity in Christ

Rooted in God's Truth

One of the most powerful gifts we can give our children is the truth of who they are in Christ. In today's world, where voices from every direction try to define identity—through social media, peer pressure, trends, or even self-doubt—our children need something stronger and more stable. That "something" is the unchanging truth of God's Word.

When we consistently teach our children what God says about them, we give them a foundation that cannot be shaken. We help them understand that their worth doesn't come from what they achieve or how they look—but from being deeply known and loved by their Creator.

As parents, it's our honor to speak life over our children. To point them to Jesus—the One who calls them chosen, set apart, dearly loved. When we declare God's Word over their lives and teach them to do the same, we're not just speaking into their present—we're shaping their future. We're planting seeds of truth that will grow into confidence, courage, and unwavering purpose.

So let these declarations become part of your daily rhythm. Say them out loud. Pray them together. Let your child repeat them with boldness. And watch as they begin to see themselves the way God sees them—fearfully and wonderfully made, secure in His love, and empowered to walk in His purpose.

Declarations

1. **Parent:** My child (insert name) is fearfully and wonderfully made by God in Jesus name. *(Psalm 139:14)*
   Child: I am fearfully and wonderfully made by God. *(Psalm 139:14)*

2. **Parent:** My child is God's workmanship, created in Christ Jesus for good works *(Ephesians 2:10)*

Child: I am God's workmanship, created for good things. *(Ephesians 2:10)*

3. **Parent:** My child is chosen, holy, and dearly loved by God *(Colossians 3:12)*
   Child: I am chosen, holy, and dearly loved. *(Colossians 3:12)*

4. **Parent:** My child is a new creation in Christ Jesus (*2 Corinthians 5:17)*
   Child: I am a new creation in Christ Jesus. *(2 Corinthians 5:17)*

5. **Parent:** I declare my child is the righteousness of God in Christ *(2 Corinthians 5:21)*
   Child: I am the righteousness of God in Christ. *(2 Corinthians 5:21)*

6. **Parent:** My child is a child of God and heir to His promises in Jesus name. *(Romans 8:16–17)*
   Child: I am a child of God and an heir with Christ. *(Romans 8:16–17)*

7. **Parent:** My child is complete in Christ, who is the head of all principalities and powers in Jesus name. *(Colossians 2:10)*
   Child: I am complete in Christ, who rules over all. *(Colossians 2:10)*

8. **Parent:** My child is the light of the world and shines for God's glory in Jesus name. *(Matthew 5:14)*
   Child: I am the light of the world, and I shine for God. *(Matthew 5:14)*

9. **Parent:** My child is more than a conqueror through Christ who loves him. *(Romans 8:37)*
   Child: I am more than a conqueror through Jesus. *(Romans 8:37)*

10. **Parent:** My child is accepted in the Beloved. *(Ephesians 1:6)*
    Child: I am accepted and loved by God. *(Ephesians 1:6)*

11. **Parent:** My child has the mind of Christ. *(1 Corinthians 2:16)*

14

Child: I have the mind of Christ. *(1 Corinthians 2:16)*

12. **Parent:** My child is redeemed and forgiven through the blood of Jesus. *(Ephesians 1:7)*
Child: I am redeemed and forgiven by Jesus' blood. *(Ephesians 1:7)*

13. **Parent:** My child is part of a chosen generation and a royal priesthood in Jesus name. *(1 Peter 2:9)*
Child: I belong to a chosen generation and a royal priesthood. *(1 Peter 2:9)*

14. **Parent:** My child is set apart for God's special purposes and he fulfills them. *(Jeremiah 1:5)*
Child: I am set apart for God's purpose. *(Jeremiah 1:5)*

15. **Parent:** My child is strong in the Lord and His mighty power in Jesus name. *(Ephesians 6:10)*
Child: I am strong in the Lord and His power. *(Ephesians 6:10)*

16. **Parent:** My child is seated in Christ in heavenly places in Jesus name. *(Ephesians 2:6)*

    Child: I am seated in Christ in heavenly places. *(Ephesians 2:6)*

17. **Parent:** My child has been called out of darkness into God's light in Jesus name. *(1 Peter 2:9)*

    Child: I've been called into God's wonderful light. *(1 Peter 2:9)*

18. **Parent:** My child is a temple of the Holy Spirit. *(1 Corinthians 6:19)*

    Child: My body is a temple of the Holy Spirit. *(1 Corinthians 6:19)*

19. **Parent:** My child walks in victory through Jesus. *(1 Corinthians 15:57)*

    Child: I have victory through Jesus. *(1 Corinthians 15:57)*

20. **Parent:** I declare that my child is rooted and grounded in God's love in Jesus name. *(Ephesians 3:17)*

Child: I am rooted and grounded in God's love. *(Ephesians 3:17)*

Reflection Questions

1. Am I speaking God's truth over my child's identity consistently?

2. What false labels or lies need to be replaced with the Word?

3. How can I show my child what it looks like to walk confidently in Christ?

4. Which declaration spoke most deeply to me today?

5. How can I make these truths part of our family's everyday conversations?

Journaling Prompt

Think of a time when you saw your child walk confidently in who God says they are. What did they do? How did you feel watching them live in that truth?

Prayer of Activation

Father, thank You for creating my child with purpose and value. I declare that no lie of the enemy will take root in their heart. Instead, let Your truth rise up and shape how they see themselves. May Your Word be the loudest voice in their life, and may they always know they are loved, accepted, and chosen by You. In Jesus' name, amen.

Practical Applications

1. **Make Daily Declarations**
   Speak 1–2 identity scriptures over your child each morning or night. It creates rhythm, connection, and spiritual stability.

2. **Use Scripture Cards**
   Write key identity declarations on index cards. Place them where your child will see them—mirror, backpack, nightstand—for daily encouragement.

3. **Practice Mirror Moments**
   Encourage your child to say one identity

statement to themselves in the mirror each day. It builds confidence and aligns their self-talk with God's Word.

4. **Engage in Story Time Reflection**
   Read Bible stories about people who embraced their identity in God (e.g., Esther, David, Paul). Discuss how your child relates to their journey.

Journal Space: Insights, Declarations, and Testimonies

_____

_____

_____

_____

_____

_____

_____

2
Purpose and Destiny

Called for a Purpose

God has created every child with a unique purpose and divine destiny. Jeremiah 1:5 reminds us that before they were formed in the womb, He knew them and set them apart for good works. As parents, we get the honor of walking alongside our children, helping them discover and embrace the unique plans God has for them.

When we speak Scriptures of purpose and destiny over our children, we plant seeds of identity and calling deep in their hearts. Each declaration reminds them they're not here by chance — they were shaped on purpose, with a purpose, destined for meaning that lasts beyond our lifetimes.

Hearing these truths regularly boosts their confidence, strengthens their ability to bounce back, and trains them to tune in to God's direction.

Children who understand they were born with intentional purpose tend to resist the pressure to just blend in or follow the crowd. As parents, our role is to water these seeds with our words and prayers, helping their vision for life take root in their spirit.

No matter where God leads them—business, arts, education, leadership, mission work—He's already planted the gifts and passions inside them to thrive in those spaces. Our job isn't to mold them after our dreams. Instead, it's to recognize what God is doing and support it—by praying it over them and speaking life into what He's already started.

And remember: purpose isn't only about what they'll do in the future. It starts with who they are today. A strong sense of identity in Christ is the foundation for everything - discipline, courage, obedience, and perseverance. Teach them to listen for God's voice, walk by faith even when the path isn't clear, and remind them that their journey is just that—an ongoing adventure with ups and downs.

Let your child know they have significance in God's plan. As they embrace their identity as God's sons and daughters, they will begin to dream boldly, serve others passionately, and live with integrity. You are raising a generation who will carry purpose forward—and the words you speak today will resound in their tomorrow.

Declarations

1. **Parent:** My child is God's masterpiece, created in Christ Jesus for good works. *(Ephesians 2:10)*
   Child: I am God's masterpiece, created in Christ Jesus for good works. *(Ephesians 2:10)*

2. **Parent:** Before my child was formed in the womb, God knew them and ordained them. *(Jeremiah 1:5)*
   Child: Before I was formed in the womb, God knew me and set me apart. *(Jeremiah 1:5)*

3. **Parent:** My child is chosen by God and called with a holy calling in Jesus name. *(2 Timothy 1:9)*

Child: I am chosen by God and called with a holy calling. *(2 Timothy 1:9)*

4. **Parent:** The plans God has for my child are for peace and a future filled with hope. *(Jeremiah 29:11)*
   Child: God's plans for me are for peace and a future filled with hope. *(Jeremiah 29:11)*

5. **Parent:** My child will fulfill the purpose for which God created them in Jesus name. *(Psalm 138:8)*
   Child: The Lord will perfect that which concerns me. *(Psalm 138:8)*

6. **Parent:** I declare my child will acknowledge the Lord in all their ways and He will direct their paths in Jesus name. *(Proverbs 3:6)*
   Child: I will acknowledge the Lord in all my ways and He will direct my paths. *(Proverbs 3:6)*

7. **Parent:** My child has an anointing from the Holy One and knows the truth in Jesus name. *(1 John 2:20)*

Child: I have an anointing from the Holy One and I know the truth. *(1 John 2:20)*

8. **Parent:** My child will be a light to their generation and glorify God in Jesus name. *(Matthew   5:14–16)*
   Child: I am the light of the world. I will let my light shine to glorify God. *(Matthew 5:14–16)*

9. **Parent:** My child will not conform to this world but be transformed by renewing their mind. (*Romans 12:2*)
   Child: I will not conform to this world but be transformed by renewing my mind. *(Romans 12:2)*

10. **Parent:** God has gifted my child with talents to serve and bless others in Jesus name. *(1 Peter 4:10)*
    Child: I have been given gifts by God to serve and bless others. *(1 Peter 4:10)*

11. **Parent:** My child's steps are ordered by the Lord, and he/she will delight in His way. *(Psalm 37:23)*

Child: My steps are ordered by the Lord, and I will delight in His way. *(Psalm 37:23)*

12. **Parent:** My child is a vessel of honor, sanctified and useful for the Master. *(2 Timothy 2:21)*

    Child: I am a vessel of honor, sanctified and useful for the Master. *(2 Timothy 2:21)*

13. **Parent:** My child will not miss their destiny or calling in Christ in Jesus name. *(Philippians 3:14)*

    Child: I press toward the goal for the prize of the upward call of God in Christ Jesus. *(Philippians 3:14)*

14. **Parent:** My child will serve the Lord with joy and fulfill their God-given assignment. *(Acts 20:24)*

    Child: I will finish my race with joy and fulfill the ministry I received from the Lord. *(Acts 20:24)*

15. **Parent:** My child has wisdom and understanding to walk in God's plan in Jesus name. *(Proverbs 2:6–7)*

Child: The Lord gives me wisdom; knowledge and understanding come from His mouth. *(Proverbs 2:6–7)*

16. **Parent:** My child flourishes like a tree planted by the rivers of water in Jesus name. *(Psalm 1:3)*
Child: I will flourish like a tree planted by the rivers of water. *(Psalm 1:3)*

17. **Parent:** I declare my child is strong and courageous, not afraid or dismayed in Jesus name. *(Joshua 1:9)*
Child: I am strong and courageous; I will not be afraid or dismayed. *(Joshua 1:9)*

18. **Parent:** God will bring to completion the good work He began in my child. *(Philippians 1:6)*
Child: God will complete the good work He began in me. *(Philippians 1:6)*

19. **Parent:** My child walks in the Spirit and bear much fruit in Jesus name. *(Galatians 5:22–23)*

Child: I will walk in the Spirit and bear the fruit of the Spirit. *(Galatians 5:22–23)*

20. **Parent:** My child will glorify God in everything they do and fulfill their kingdom assignment in Jesus name. *(Colossians 3:17)*

    Child: I will glorify God in all I do and fulfill my kingdom purpose. *(Colossians 3:17)*

Reflection Questions

1. What specific gifts or talents do I see in my child that reflect God's purpose?

2. How can I encourage my child to seek God for direction in their life?

3. Am I intentionally speaking life and purpose over my child daily?

4. What fears do I need to release about my child's future and destiny?

5. How can I help my child understand their identity in Christ more deeply?

Journaling Prompt

Reflect on a moment when you sensed God's unique calling on your child's life. Write about how that moment affirmed their purpose and how you can nurture it going forward.

Prayer of Activation

Father, thank You for creating my child with divine intention and purpose. I believe they are not here by accident but for such a time as this. Help me steward their gifts well and root my words in truth each day. May they grow in confidence as they embrace their identity in You. Lead them, Holy Spirit, down paths of righteousness and reveal the plans You've laid out for them. Soften their heart to hear Your voice and give them courage to follow. In Jesus' name, amen.

Practical Applications

1. **Identity & Purpose Affirmation Board**
   Work with your child to build a purpose board filled with scriptures, encouraging words, and images representing their strengths and

dreams. Keep it somewhere visible and update it regularly.

2. **Monthly Purpose Conversations**
   Have a standing date each month—just you and your child—to talk about their identity and calling. Ask thoughtful questions like, "What are you passionate about?" or "How do you feel God might be using you?" These conversations nurture their spiritual awareness and sense of confidence.

3. **Purpose-Filled Prayer Journal**
   Encourage your child to start a simple journal where they write down prayers, dreams, or things they believe God is speaking to them. Help them reflect on how God is shaping their identity and purpose over time. Revisit the journal together periodically to celebrate growth and answered prayers.

4. **Serve Together with Purpose**
   Find small ways to serve others as a family—whether it's volunteering, making care packages, or writing encouraging notes. Talk

with your child about how serving helps us live out our God-given purpose and discover our gifts in action. This builds empathy and reinforces their calling to impact others for God's glory.

Journal Space: Insights, Declarations, and Testimonies

_____

_____

_____

_____

_____

_____

_____

3
Wisdom and Guidance

The Lord Gives Wisdom

In a world filled with noisy opinions, ever-changing morals, and constant pressure to conform, our children don't just need information —they need true wisdom that comes from above. The kind of wisdom that doesn't shift with trends or emotions. Scripture tells us plainly that *"Wisdom is the principal thing; therefore get wisdom"* (Proverbs 4:7). It's not optional—it's essential.

Godly wisdom acts like a compass for our children. It shapes how they view the world, how they make decisions, and how they understand what honors God and what doesn't. When our children grow in wisdom, they're not just learning facts—they're learning how to live rightly, love deeply, and stand firmly in truth no matter what comes their way. When children learn to seek and apply wisdom, they develop the ability to navigate challenges and stay focused on the path God has laid out for them. In this way, wisdom not only shapes their purpose but also helps bring their destiny to fruition with patience and faithfulness.

As parents, it's our privilege—and our responsibility—to pray for wisdom over our children and to speak it into their lives every day. When we declare God's Word over them, we're not just reciting verses. We are helping align their hearts with heaven's perspective. We're helping them hear God's voice above the noise and develop the kind of discernment that lasts a lifetime.

The more our children hear us declare truth over them, the more likely they are to internalize it. As they begin to speak those same truths over themselves, it becomes more than head knowledge —it becomes heart knowledge. That foundation of wisdom will serve them in school, in friendships, in future careers, and in every relationship.

So don't underestimate the power of your words. Let your declarations be filled with faith, and invite your children to join in. This is how we build a legacy of wisdom—one declaration, one decision, one conversation at a time.

Declarations

1. **Parent:** My child receives wisdom and understanding from the Lord, who gives generously and never withholds what is good *(Proverbs 2:6)*
   Child: I receive wisdom and understanding from God, and He leads me in what is right. *(Proverbs 2:6)*

2. **Parent:** My child puts their full trust in the Lord and doesn't rely on their own limited view. *(Proverbs 3:5)*
   Child: I trust God with all my heart and won't depend on just what I understand. *(Proverbs 3:5)*

3. **Parent:** God orders my child's steps, and their plans are established in Him. *(Proverbs 16:9)*
   Child: The Lord directs my steps, and He

helps me walk in His perfect way. *(Proverbs 16:9)*

4. **Parent:** My child is taught directly by the Lord, and that teaching brings lasting peace. *(Isaiah 54:13)*
   Child: I am taught by the Lord, and His truth gives me peace that stays. *(Isaiah 54:13)*

5. **Parent:** My child hears the leading of the Holy Spirit and responds with obedience in Jesus name. *(John 16:13)*
   Child: I listen to the Holy Spirit, and He leads me into all truth. *(John 16:13)*

6. **Parent:** Just like Jesus, my child grows in wisdom, maturity, and favor with God and people. *(Luke 2:52)*
   Child: I grow in wisdom and maturity, and I find favor with both God and others. *(Luke 2:52)*

7. **Parent:** My child has the mind of Christ and thinks with clarity and purpose. *(1 Corinthians 2:16)*
   Child: I have the mind of Christ and can think

clearly with His truth guiding me. *(1 Corinthians 2:16)*

8. **Parent:** My child reveres the Lord, and that holy fear is the very beginning of wisdom in their life in Jesus name *(Proverbs 9:10)*
   Child: I honor the Lord with deep respect, and that's where wisdom begins for me. *(Proverbs 9:10)*

9. **Parent:** My child is filled with spiritual wisdom and revelation to know God deeply. *(Ephesians 1:17)*
   Child: I am full of wisdom and revelation because I know who God is and He shows me more. *(Ephesians 1:17)*

10. **Parent:** My child seeks the Lord's counsel in every decision and follows His voice with confidence in Jesus name. *(Psalm 32:8)*
    Child: I ask God for guidance, and He shows me which path to take. *(Psalm 32:8)*

11. **Parent:** My child walks wisely, using their time and choices well in Jesus name *(Ephesians 5:15)*

Child: I walk with wisdom and use my time wisely, making the most of every moment. *(Ephesians 5:15)*

12. **Parent:** My child's plans and thoughts are established in the Lord as they commit everything to Him in Jesus name. *(Proverbs 16:3)*
    Child: I commit my ways to God, and He establishes my thoughts and plans. *(Proverbs 16:3)*

13. **Parent:** My child treasures God's Word and meditates on it throughout the day and night in Jesus name. *(Psalm 1:2)*
    Child: I love God's Word and think about it all day and night. *(Psalm 1:2)*

14. **Parent:** My child isn't puffed up by their own wisdom but walks in humility and fear of the Lord in Jesus name. *(Proverbs 3:7)*
    Child: I don't depend on my own wisdom. I humble myself, fear the Lord, and depart from evil. *(Proverbs 3:7)*

15. Parent: My child's heart is equipped to discern between what is good and what is evil. *(1 Kings 3:9)*
Child: God gives me a heart that can tell right from wrong and choose what pleases Him. *(1 Kings 3:9)*

16. Parent: God's Word lights my child's path and helps them navigate life with clarity. *(Psalm 119:105)*
Child: God's Word is a lamp showing me where to go. *(Psalm 119:105)*

17. Parent: My child surrounds themselves with wise people and becomes wise through those connections. *(Proverbs 13:20)*
Child: I choose to walk with wise people, and I become wiser because of it. *(Proverbs 13:20)*

18. Parent: God gives my child wisdom and insight beyond their years in Jesus name. *(Daniel 1:17)*
Child: God gives me understanding and

knowledge beyond what I've learned on my own. *(Daniel 1:17)*

19. Parent: The Lord orders every step my child takes and delights in the journey He has for them. *(Psalm 37:23)*
Child: My steps are guided by the Lord, and He takes joy in my path. *(Psalm 37:23)*

20. Parent: The Holy Spirit teaches my child everything they need to know and reminds them of truth at the right time in Jesus name. *(John 14:26)*
Child: The Holy Spirit teaches me and helps me remember the truth exactly when I need it. *(John 14:26)*

Reflection Questions

1. Am I modeling wise choices in a way that my child can observe and learn from?

2. Do I regularly invite God's wisdom into our home, our routines, and our parenting?

3. What can I do to help my child recognize the Holy Spirit's voice and guidance?

4. Where might I need to grow in discernment so I can lead my child better?

5. Which scripture about wisdom stands out to me today, and why?

Journaling Prompt

Write out a personal prayer asking God to fill your child with wisdom. Be honest and specific—what areas do you see them struggling with, and where do you hope to see them grow? Invite God into that space.

Prayer of Activation

Lord, You are the fountain of all wisdom, and I praise You for being faithful to lead and guide us. I ask You today to fill my child with Your wisdom. Let their heart be sensitive to Your voice and their spirit open to Your truth. Teach them to value Your Word, seek Your counsel, and walk in discernment. Guide their every step and help them grow in wisdom all their days.

In Jesus' name, amen.

Practical Applications

1. **Wisdom Verse of the Week**
   Choose one Bible verse about wisdom each week to memorize as a family. Reflect on it together throughout the week, discussing how it applies in daily decisions.

2. **Decision-Making Journal**
   Encourage your child to keep a journal where they can write down decisions they're facing. Guide them in praying over each one, and review it later to see how God answered or led them.

3. **"Ask God First" Habit**
   Teach your child the simple but powerful habit of pausing to pray before making any decision—even small ones. Let them experience that asking God first leads to better outcomes.

4. **Surround with Wisdom**
   Help your child build strong friendships with others who also seek God. Encourage mentorship from wise adults like youth

leaders, teachers, or extended family who model a life of wisdom and integrity.

Journal Space: Insights, Declarations, and Testimonies

_____

_____

_____

_____

_____

_____

_____

_____

_____

_____

4
Protection and Safety

God Our Defender

When children feel protected—emotionally, spiritually, and physically—they're better able to grow into the purpose God has placed on their lives. That sense of security helps guard them from the harmful voices and experiences in the world that could otherwise pull them off course.

We live in uncertain times, and as parents, one of our deepest desires is to protect our children. Whether it's from physical danger, emotional pain, or spiritual attacks, we feel the weight of that responsibility. But here's the comforting truth: God loves our children even more than we do, and His promises to protect them are strong and dependable.

Psalm 91 is often called the "protection chapter." It reminds us that when we choose to dwell in

God's presence, we are covered by His shadow. His Word assures us that His angels are assigned to watch over our children. When we speak these promises, we're not just offering comfort—we're activating spiritual protection that surrounds them like a shield.

Every time you declare these scriptures, you're stepping into your role as a spiritual watchman over your home. Whether your children are toddlers or teens, God's promise stands firm: He is their protector. So declare these truths with confidence, trust in His faithfulness, and find peace in knowing that the One who watches over your children never sleeps.

Declarations

1. **Parent**: My child dwells in the secret place of the Most High and abides under the shadow of the Almighty in Jesus name. (Psalm 91:1)
   Child: I am covered by God. (Psalm 91:1)

2. **Parent**: No evil shall befall my child, nor shall any plague come near their dwelling. (Psalm 91:10)

Child: No harm will come near me or my home. (Psalm 91:10)

3. **Parent**: God has given His angels charge over my child to keep them in all their ways. (Psalm 91:11)
   Child: God sends His angels to protect me everywhere I go. (Psalm 91:11)

4. **Parent**: The Lord is a shield around my child, their glory and the lifter of their head in Jesus name. (Psalm 3:3)
   Child: God is my shield and my protector. (Psalm 3:3)

5. **Parent**: The Lord preserves my child's going out and coming in in Jesus name. (Psalm 121:8)
   Child: The Lord keeps me safe when I go out and when I come in. (Psalm 121:8)

6. **Parent**: My child is hidden in Christ, safe from every scheme of the enemy in Jesus name. (Colossians 3:3)
   Child: I am hidden with Christ and safe from all harm. (Colossians 3:3)

7. **Parent**: No weapon formed against my child shall prosper. (Isaiah 54:17)
Child: No weapon formed against me will succeed. (Isaiah 54:17)

8. **Parent**: The blood of Jesus covers and protects my child. (Exodus 12:13)
Child: I am covered by the blood of Jesus. (Exodus 12:13)

9. **Parent**: My child is surrounded by God's favor and protection like a shield in Jesus name. (Psalm 5:12)
Child: God's favor and protection surround me like a shield. (Psalm 5:12)

10. **Parent**: The Lord is a strong tower for my child; he/she runs to Him and is safe in Jesus name.   (Proverbs 18:10)
Child: The Lord is my safe place, and I am not afraid. (Proverbs 18:10)

11. **Parent**: My child walks securely for he/she walks in wisdom in Jesus name. (Proverbs 3:23)

Child: I walk safely because God gives me wisdom. (Proverbs 3:23)

12. **Parent**: God is my child's refuge and fortress in Jesus name. (Psalm 91:2)
    Child: God is my place of safety and strength. (Psalm 91:2)

13. **Parent**: The Lord delivers my child from every snare and peril. (Psalm 91:3)
    Child: God saves me from every trap. (Psalm 91:3)

14. **Parent**: My child will not fear the terror by night or the arrow by day in Jesus name. (Psalm 91:5)
    Child: I do not fear the night or the day. (Psalm 91:5)

15. **Parent**: A thousand may fall at their side, but no harm shall come near them n Jesus name. (Psalm 91:7)
    Child: Trouble may come near others, but I will be protected. (Psalm 91:7)

16. Parent: The sun shall not strike my child by day, nor the moon by night in Jesus name. (Psalm 121:6)
Child: God watches over me all day and night. (Psalm 121:6)

17. Parent: God protects my child from all evil. (Psalm 121:7)
Child: The Lord keeps me safe from all harm. (Psalm 121:7)

18. Parent: My child is guarded by the Lord, who never sleeps nor slumbers in Jesus name. (Psalm 121:4)
Child: God never stops watching over me. (Psalm 121:4)

19. Parent: The Lord places a hedge of protection around my child. (Job 1:10)
Child: God has built a wall of protection around me. (Job 1:10)

20. Parent: My child lives under the banner of the Lord's love in Jesus name. (Song of Solomon 2:4)

Child: I live under God's banner of love and peace. (Song of Solomon 2:4)

Reflection Questions

1. In what areas do I truly trust God to protect my child?

2. Are there any fears I need to hand over to God today?

3. Have I declared God's promises of safety over my children this week?

4. How can I teach my child to rely on God for protection?

5. Which verses bring me the most peace when I'm worried about my child?

Journaling Prompt

Think back to a time when you saw God protect your child or your family. What happened? How did it grow your faith?

Prayer of Activation

Lord, thank You for being our refuge and protector. I entrust my child into Your care, knowing that You never sleep or turn away. Cover them with Your presence and shield them from harm. I silence every fear and anxiety in my heart and speak peace and protection over my child today. Surround them with angels and let Your Word be a wall of fire around them. In Jesus' name, amen.

Practical Application

1. **Create and Practice a Daily "Protection Prayer" Routine**
    Start each morning or end each night by reading Psalm 91 together as a family. Let your child speak it over themselves, helping them memorize God's promises.

2. **Post Scripture Cards as Reminders**
    Write out key verses on cards and place them in your child's room, school bag, or lunchbox. These visible reminders help keep

God's protection top of mind throughout their day.

Journal Space: Insights, Declarations, and Testimonies

_____

_____

_____

_____

_____

_____

_____

_____

_____

_____

5
Family and Relationships

The Heart of Family

A child's understanding of who they are and why they're here begins in the relationships that surround them. Within the family, children first encounter love, correction, belonging, and trust—core experiences that shape their sense of identity. When they know they are deeply loved and seen, not just by their parents but by God, they begin to carry that identity with confidence. And it's through those same relationships that a child starts to discover purpose—not as something distant or abstract, but as something lived out daily in how they treat others, serve, and contribute. In this way, family becomes more than a place to grow up—it becomes the soil where identity is rooted and purpose begins to grow.

Family is one of God's most beautiful and intentional gifts. It's not just a social structure—

it's the very first place where children are meant to experience what it means to love and be loved, to respect and be respected, and to walk in unity with others. It's within the walls of the home that the deepest lessons of grace, kindness, and relationship begin to take root.

The Bible reminds us that honoring our parents, forgiving one another, and living in peace are not just good suggestions—they are part of God's design for how we're meant to relate to each other (see Ephesians 6:1–4; Colossians 3:13–14). When family relationships are nurtured in love and built on Christ-like principles, they become the foundation for every future relationship our children will form.

As parents, we are called to cultivate an environment where love leads, forgiveness flows freely, respect is mutual, and unity is cherished. It's in this sacred space that our children learn not only how to treat others, but also how to carry the love of Jesus into the world. Speaking God's Word over our families isn't just about quoting scripture

—it's about releasing peace, purpose, and protection into the atmosphere of our homes.

When children hear words of blessing spoken over them—words rooted in truth and God's promises —they begin to internalize those truths. And as they learn to declare them over themselves, they grow in confidence, compassion, and clarity about what healthy relationships should look like. These seeds of truth take root and grow into resilience and emotional health that will carry them through every season of life.

Encourage your child not only to receive these declarations but to speak them aloud with boldness and faith. As they do, they're not just forming habits—they're forming a strong foundation for lifelong, God-honoring relationships.

Declarations

1. **Parent:** My child loves and honors their parents, obeying as the Lord instructs in Jesus name. *(Ephesians 6:1)*
   Child: I love and honor my parents, and I

choose to obey them as God teaches. *(Ephesians 6:1)*

2. **Parent:** My child enjoys peace and unity within our home and family in Jesus name. *(Psalm 133:1)*

   Child: I experience peace and unity in my family, and I'm thankful for it. *(Psalm 133:1)*

3. **Parent:** My child shows patience and kindness in how they relate to their siblings and friends in Jesus name. *(1 Corinthians 13:4)*

   Child: I am patient and kind when I interact with my siblings and friends. *(1 Corinthians 13:4)*

4. **Parent:** My child forgives others freely, just as Christ has forgiven them. *(Colossians 3:13)*

   Child: I choose to forgive others because Jesus forgave me. *(Colossians 3:13)*

5. **Parent:** My child forms strong friendships built on mutual respect and love. *(Proverbs 17:17)*

Child: I build friendships that are respectful, loving, and God-honoring. *(Proverbs 17:17)*

6. **Parent:** My child is a peacemaker, offering grace and wisdom in times of conflict in Jesus name. *(Matthew 5:9)*
   Child: I am a peacemaker who brings calm and grace when there's conflict. *(Matthew 5:9)*

7. **Parent:** My child respects our guidance and chooses obedience with a willing heart. *(Ephesians 6:1)*
   Child: I respect and obey my parents, trusting their love and wisdom. *(Ephesians 6:1)*

8. **Parent:** My child's words bring life, encouragement, and truth in Jesus name. *(Ephesians 4:29)*
   Child: My words lift others up and speak truth from my heart. *(Ephesians 4:29)*

9. **Parent:** My child loves others deeply, the same way Jesus loves them in Jesus name. *(John 13:34)*

Child: I love people the way Jesus loves me — with compassion and care. *(John 13:34)*

10. **Parent:** My child honors leaders and those in authority with respect in Jesus name. *(Romans 13:1)*
    Child: I show honor and respect to my leaders and those in authority. *(Romans 13:1)*

11. **Parent:** My child is a blessing—not only to our family but to the entire community in Jesus name. *(Genesis 12:2)*
    Child: God makes me a great nation. I am a blessing to my family and the people around me. *(Genesis 12:2)*

12. **Parent:** My child acts with kindness, mercy, and trust in every relationship. *(Proverbs 3:3)*
    Child: I am kind and trustworthy in all my relationships in Jesus name. *(Proverbs 3:3)*

13. **Parent:** I declare my child is humble and gentle in how they treat others *(Philippians 2:3)*
    Child: I treat others with gentleness and walk in humility. *(Philippians 2:3)*

14. Parent: My child defends and cares for those who are vulnerable or in need in Jesus name. *(Psalm 82:3)*
Child: I care for people who need help and stand up for those who can't. *(Psalm 82:3)*

15. Parent: My child is honest and speaks truth with love and wisdom in Jesus name. *(Ephesians 4:15)*
Child: I tell the truth in love and choose honesty in all things. *(Ephesians 4:15)*

16. Parent: My child is patient when waiting and kind when helping others. *(Galatians 5:22)*
Child: I wait patiently and help others with kindness. *(Galatians 5:22)*

17. Parent: My child regularly shows thankfulness and expresses appreciation. *(1 Thessalonians 5:18)*
Child: I am thankful and show appreciation to those around me. *(1 Thessalonians 5:18)*

18. Parent: My child's heart is open to healing, restoration, and reconciliation. *(Matthew 6:14)*

Child: I welcome healing and forgive quickly, just like Jesus taught me. *(Matthew 6:14)*

19. **Parent:** Our family dwells under God's protection and rests in His presence in Jesus name. *(Psalm 91:1–2)*
    Child: My family is safe under God's protection and we rest in Him. *(Psalm 91:1–2)*

20. **Parent:** I declare my child walks in humility and puts others before themselves with honor in Jesus name. *(Philippians 2:3)*
    Child: I walk humbly and treat others with honor, putting them before myself. *(Philippians 2:3)*

Reflection Questions

1. How am I showing love and respect in my own family relationships?

2. What are some ways I can help my child become a peacemaker in everyday situations?

3. Are there relationships in our home that need healing through God's grace?

4. How can I model forgiveness and patience more consistently in my interactions?

5. What small but powerful steps can our family take this week to grow in unity?

Journaling Prompt

Think back on a recent moment within your family —whether a joyful one or a challenging one. How was God's love shown, or how could it have been shown more clearly? What would you want to improve or do differently next time?

Prayer of Activation

Heavenly Father, thank You for the priceless gift of family. I ask that You help us grow in love, patience, and unity every day. Let forgiveness come easily and encouragement overflow in our home. Help my child to love deeply, serve joyfully, and walk in Your truth in every relationship. May our home be a place where Your presence dwells and Your peace reigns. Bind our hearts together with Your unbreakable love. In Jesus' name, amen.

Practical Applications

1. **Family Night Devotion**
   Meet every evening each week to come together as a family for devotion. You can choose a verse on love, forgiveness, or unity, and discuss what it means to each person. End with prayer and declarations.

2. **Encourage Apologies and Restoration**
   Create a culture where saying "I'm sorry" and "I forgive you" is normal and safe. Let your children see you model this first. Teach them that mistakes don't break love—they become opportunities for growth and healing.

3. **Positive Communication Challenge**
   For one week, challenge everyone in the family to only speak words that uplift. At the end of the week, reflect together on how your home felt with positive words as the norm.

4. **Serve Together as a Family**
   Choose small acts of service—whether it's writing notes of encouragement, helping a neighbor, or volunteering as a family. Serving

others together strengthens family bonds and reinforces the heart of Christ.

Journal Space: Insights, Declarations, and Testimonies

_____

_____

_____

_____

_____

_____

_____

_____

_____

_____

6
Practical Tools for Kingdom Families

Equipping the Family for Kingdom Living

A flourishing, Christ-centered family doesn't come together by accident. It's built with love, care, and consistent intentionality. It takes time, prayer, and a willingness to invest in both spiritual rhythms and practical habits that strengthen your home from the inside out. When families purposefully nurture their walk with God and with each other, they reflect the beauty of God's design —and lay the groundwork for a legacy of faith that will impact generations to come.

God's Word is the firm foundation for everything we do. In our everyday choices—like prayer time, shared worship, bible studies, encouraging conversations, and family time and culture—we have the opportunity to strengthen that foundation. These moments shape the atmosphere of your home and infuse it with peace, purpose, and joy. When you teach your children how to engage with God through scripture, worship, and prayer—not just during Sunday services, but throughout the week—you're building a spiritual habit that becomes a lifeline through every season of life.

Integrating spiritual tools and faith-centered practices into your family's daily routine helps ensure that faith isn't just a set of beliefs—it becomes a lifestyle that is lived out. It turns your home into a place where God's presence is felt deeply, and where every family member is empowered to grow in their calling, identity, and relationship with Christ. These tools give your children practical ways to encounter God personally and to learn how to walk with Him faithfully.

Declarations

1. **Parent:** Our family is built on the solid rock of Jesus Christ. We will not be shaken, no matter what comes. *(Matthew 7:24–25)*

   Child: I build my life on the rock of Jesus

Christ, and I stand strong in Him. *(Matthew 7:24–25)*

2. **Parent:** God's Word lights the path ahead for our family and shows us the way to walk. *(Psalm 119:105)*
   Child: God's Word guides my steps and lights up my path. *(Psalm 119:105)*

3. **Parent:** We are a praying family—consistent, faithful, and empowered by the Holy Spirit. *(1 Thessalonians 5:17)*
   Child: I pray without stopping, and God strengthens me through His Spirit. *(1 Thessalonians 5:17)*

4. **Parent:** The peace of Christ rules in every room of our home and in each of our hearts. *(Colossians 3:15)*
   Child: Christ's peace fills my heart and my life with calm and confidence. *(Colossians 3:15)*

5. **Parent:** Our family chooses words that encourage, uplift, and speak life in Jesus name. *(Ephesians 4:29)*

Child: I use words that build others up and bring encouragement. *(Ephesians 4:29)*

6. **Parent:** The joy of the Lord fills our home and gives us strength each day in Jesus name *(Nehemiah 8:10)*
Child: God's joy gives me strength and fills my heart with delight. *(Nehemiah 8:10)*

7. **Parent:** I declare our home is a place of healing, forgiveness, and grace in Jesus name. *(Ephesians 4:32)*
Child: I choose to forgive and live with grace and kindness. *(Ephesians 4:32)*

8. **Parent:** We are united in love and purpose, growing stronger together in Christ. *(Ephesians 4:16)*
Child: I am connected to my family in love and growing together in Jesus. *(Ephesians 4:16)*

9. **Parent:** I declare everything we do and say honors the name of Jesus in Jesus name. *(Colossians 3:17)*

Child: I choose to honor God with my words and actions every day. *(Colossians 3:17)*

10. **Parent:** We serve one another with joyful hearts and humble hands in Jesus name. *(Galatians 5:13)*
    Child: I serve others with joy and a heart full of love. *(Galatians 5:13)*

11. **Parent:** God's blessing and favor rest on our family today and every day in Jesus name. *(Psalm 128:5–6)*
    Child: God blesses me and surrounds me with His favor always. *(Psalm 128:5–6)*

12. **Parent:** Our family lives by faith, walks in hope, and overflows with love in Jesus name. *(1 Corinthians 13:13)*
    Child: I live in faith, I walk in hope, and I love with all my heart. *(1 Corinthians 13:13)*

13. **Parent:** Our hearts are woven together in harmony and peace through God. *(Philippians 2:2)*
    Child: God fills my heart with peace and

connects me to others in love. *(Philippians 2:2)*

14. **Parent:** The Lord surrounds our family with His favor and protection like a mighty shield in Jesus name. *(Psalm 5:12)*
    Child: God protects me and surrounds me with His favor like a strong shield. *(Psalm 5:12)*

15. **Parent:** We stand firm in our faith, bold and courageous through every storm in Jesus name. *(1 Corinthians 16:13)*
    Child: I stand strong in faith and live with courage and boldness. *(1 Corinthians 16:13)*

16. **Parent:** Our home is filled with the presence and peace of God in Jesus name. *(Psalm 84:10)*
    Child: God's presence is with me, and His peace fills my life. *(Psalm 84:10)*

17. **Parent:** We teach our children to love God with all their heart, soul, and mind. *(Deuteronomy 6:5)*

Child: I love the Lord with all my heart, all my soul, and all my mind. *(Deuteronomy 6:5)*

18. **Parent:** We live with open hands—ready to give, ready to receive, and full of God's generosity. *(Acts 20:35)*
    Child: I live with an open heart and open hands, giving and receiving God's blessings. *(Acts 20:35)*

19. **Parent:** Our family walks in humility, showing honor and love to one another. *(Romans 12:10)*
    Child: I walk humbly and put others before myself in love. *(Romans 12:10)*

20. **Parent:** God's grace empowers us to grow daily in love, truth, and maturity in Jesus name. *(2 Peter 3:18)*
    Child: I grow in God's grace, knowledge, love, truth, and strength. *(2 Peter 3:18)*

Reflection Questions

1. What spiritual practices do we already follow together as a family?

68

2. How can we improve our daily rhythms to make room for God's presence?

3. Which spiritual habits have been most impactful in shaping our family culture?

4. In what ways do I model faith and devotion to my children?

5. What new routines or tools could we add to deepen our family's relationship with God?

Journaling Prompt

Think of a time when a spiritual practice—like family prayer, worship, or scripture reading— brought your family closer together or closer to God. What made that moment so special? How can you create more of those moments?

Prayer of Activation

Lord God, thank You for the gift of family and the tools You've given us to build a strong, faith-filled home. Help us to be intentional in our spiritual habits and to keep You at the center of our daily lives. Strengthen the bonds between us, and fill our home with Your love, joy, and peace. May

Your Word be our guide, Your Spirit our teacher, and Your grace our strength. Let our home be a place where Your presence is welcomed, honored, and celebrated.

In Jesus' name, amen.

Practical Applications

1. Establish a Family Devotional Time
Choose a regular time daily for a shared devotional. Include Bible reading, prayer, and worship. Make it engaging and age-appropriate for everyone in the family.

2. Create a Family Prayer Wall or Jar
Set up a visible space in your home where everyone can write down prayer requests and testimonies. Review and pray over them regularly. Celebrate when prayers are answered.

3. Encourage Journaling for Spiritual Growth
Help your children start a personal faith journal. Let them record their prayers, Bible verses that speak to them, and moments where they saw God move in their lives.

4. **Celebrate Spiritual Milestones Together**
   Acknowledge moments like a child's first prayer, baptism, or when they share a word from God. Celebrate these milestones to show them that faith is something worth honoring.

Journal Space: Insights, Declarations, and Testimonies

_____

_____

_____

_____

_____

_____

_____

_____

Conclusion: Building a Legacy That Lasts

As you come to the close of this journey through intentional spiritual parenting, take a moment to reflect on the sacred calling you carry. Raising a family in God's truth isn't just about discipline, structure, or tradition—it's about sowing seeds of faith that will bloom across generations. You are shaping more than just behavior; you are raising sons and daughters of the King—heirs to His promises, carriers of His presence, and ambassadors of His love.

Every word of life you've spoken over your children, every time you've chosen to trust God in the hard moments, and every act of selfless love you've poured out has mattered more than you know. These are not small things—they are the building blocks of a spiritual legacy that will echo far beyond your lifetime. While the road of intentional parenting is not always smooth or easy, the fruit it bears is eternal: children who know who they are in Christ, homes marked by peace and purpose, and families rooted deeply in God's presence.

God's design for the family is both beautiful and powerful. When we anchor ourselves in His Word, lean on His wisdom, and use the practical tools He's given us, our homes become living expressions of His kingdom on earth. Your role as a parent is not ordinary—it is holy. It is a divine partnership with God to nurture the hearts and futures of those He has placed in your care.

So keep going. Keep declaring the promises of God even when you don't see immediate fruit. Keep walking by faith, even on the days when you feel weak. Keep inviting the Holy Spirit into every room of your home and every decision you make. You are not alone in this—God is with you, and He is faithful to complete the good work He started in your family.

May your household shine with His light and be a living testimony of what it means to follow Jesus. May your children rise up, strong in identity and purpose, firm in truth, and full of grace and wisdom. And may your family story be one that reflects the glory and goodness of God in every season.

Final Encouragement

Let this book remain close to your heart as you continue walking this path of purposeful parenting. Revisit the declarations often. Meditate on the scriptures. Reapply the teachings and practical applications as your family grows. Each time you return to these pages, let the Holy Spirit breathe new life into your parenting journey.

You don't have to have it all figured out. What matters most is that you keep showing up, rooted in God's love and reliant on His strength. Trust that He will equip you, sustain you, and surround your family with His presence every step of the way.

Closing Prayer
Father,

Thank You for the incredible gift and calling of parenthood. Thank You for trusting us with Your children and inviting us to partner with You in shaping their hearts and futures. Lord, we ask for Your wisdom to lead with grace, Your strength to parent with love, and Your Spirit to guide us daily.

Fill our homes with Your peace. Let forgiveness flow freely, and let joy run deep. Make our homes places of healing, honor, truth, and hope. Help us raise children who love You wholeheartedly, who walk in Your ways, and who shine brightly in this world.

Establish our families in Your truth, protect us under Your wings, and empower us by Your Spirit to leave a legacy that glorifies You. In all things, may we reflect Your heart and carry Your light. In Jesus' name, amen.

Resources for Your Family

For Printable Family Declarations and other resources, go to whollybooks.com
Other books by the author and contact.

Other books by the author include:

1. Intentional Spiritual Parenting
2. Declarations to Speak Life Over Your Children — Nurturing Identity, Purpose, and Wisdom Through God's Word
3. Declarations to Speak Life Over Your Children — Nurturing Wellness, Courage, and Character Through God's Word
4. Declarations to Speak Life Over Your Children — Nurturing Leadership Impact and Authority in the Seven Mountains of Influence Through God's Word

Go to whollybooks.com for more information on books by the author. You can find our books at all your favorite bookstores and online retailers.

Additional Information

About the Author

Christy Ojikutu is passionate about equipping parents to raise world-changers through the power of prayer, Scripture, and intentional parenting. With a heart for families and a love for God's Word, she believes that what we speak over our children today will echo through eternity.

Thank You

Thank you for taking this journey of intentional parenting through the power of God's Word. Your dedication to speak life over your children is sowing seeds that will flourish for generations to come. May every declaration fill your home with God's presence, peace, and promises fulfilled. Let's continue building faith-filled families together!

www.ingramcontent.com/pod-product-compliance
Lightning Source LLC
Chambersburg PA
CBHW060349050426
42449CB00011B/2900